I0436195

Visit Our Website To Learn More!

You can find additional information about ERS publications, databases, and other products at our website.

www.ers.usda.gov

National Agricultural Library Cataloging Record:

Gale, Fred
Imports from China and food safety issues.
(Economic information bulletin; no. 52)

  1. Food industry and trade—China.
  2. Food adulteration and inspection—United States.
  3. Food handling—China.
  4. Imports—United States.
  I. Buzby, Jean C.
 II. United States. Dept. of Agriculture. Economic Research Service.
 III. Title.

HD9000.9.U5

Photo credit: Fred Gale, USDA/ERS

United States
Department
of Agriculture

Economic
Information
Bulletin
Number 52

July 2009

A Report from the Economic Research Service

www.ers.usda.gov

Imports From China and Food Safety Issues

Fred Gale, fgale@ers.usda.gov
Jean C. Buzby, jbuzby@ers.usda.gov

Abstract

The U.S. Food and Drug Administration's (FDA) increased attention to food imports from China is an indicator of safety concerns as imported food becomes more common in the United States. U.S. food imports from China more than tripled in value between 2001 and 2008. Addressing safety risks associated with these imports is difficult because of the vast array of products from China, China's weak enforcement of food safety standards, its heavy use of agricultural chemicals, and its considerable environmental pollution. FDA import refusal data highlight food safety problems that appear to recur in trade and where FDA has focused its import alerts and monitoring efforts. FDA refusals of food shipments from China suggest recurring problems with "filth," unsafe additives, labeling (typically introduced in food processing and handling), and veterinary drug residues in fish and shellfish (introduced at the farm). Chinese authorities try to control food export safety by certifying exporters and the farms that supply them. However, monitoring such a wide range of products for the different hazards that can arise at varying points in the supply chain is a difficult challenge for Chinese and U.S. officials.

Keywords: China, food imports, food safety, U.S. Food and Drug Administration, FDA, misbranding, labeling, refusals, shipment, violation.

Acknowledgments

We would like to thank ERS interns Shariyar Zarea and Andrew Anderson-Sprecher for their contributions to this project in data analysis and reviews of literature and regulations on Chinese food safety. We received helpful review comments on the manuscript from Geoff Becker, Congressional Research Service; Larry Busch, Michigan State University; Linda Calvin, ERS; Christopher J. Hickey, FDA; and Mark Petry, USDA's Foreign Agricultural Service. This study benefited from information obtained from ERS trips to China supported by USDA's scientific exchange program in 2006 and 2007 to assess food safety.

Contents

Recommended citation format for this publication:

Gale, Fred, and Jean C. Buzby, *Imports From China and Food Safety Issues*, Economic Information Bulletin No. 52, U.S. Department of Agriculture, Economic Research Service, July 2009.

Summary

Rising consumption of imported food poses challenges for U.S. food safety officials. Retailers and processors seeking low-cost suppliers and exotic and ethnic foods demanded by U.S. consumers procure foods and ingredients all over the globe. It is often difficult to ensure that suppliers in far-flung locations operate according to the high safety standards and tight quality control sought by U.S. consumers.

What Is the Issue?

China has emerged in recent years as an important source of food imports in the United States. Food imports from China more than tripled in value between 2001 and 2008. Several highly publicized incidents of food contamination and adulteration in both the Chinese food supply and in U.S. food imports from China have focused public concern on the safety of food from China. Motivated in part by these concerns, a U.S. Government Interagency Working Group on Import Safety issued an *Action Plan for Import Safety* and the U.S. Food and Drug Administration (FDA) issued a *Food Protection Plan* in 2007. FDA opened its first overseas office in China in 2008.

This report discusses potential food safety risks associated with food imports from China based on available data. The report describes the types of foods imported from China based on U.S. Customs statistics and assesses their importance in the U.S. food supply, analyzes FDA refusals of food shipments from China, and describes food safety regulation and enforcement in China. Although the FDA data do not necessarily reflect the distribution of risk in foods, the import refusal data highlight food safety concerns for which FDA has focused its import alerts, examinations (e.g., sampling), and other monitoring efforts.

What Did the Study Find?

The increase in U.S. food safety concerns is partly a result of the recent increase in global food trade. China is one of the fastest growing sources of U.S. food imports. In 2008, the value of food imports from China reached $5.2 billion, making China the third-largest source of food imports. About 41 percent of this import value was from fish and seafood, most of it farm-raised. Juices and pickled, dried, and canned vegetables and fruit accounted for another 25 percent. The remainder included a wide variety of products, many associated with Asian cuisine.

Despite the rapid growth, less than 1 percent of the U.S. food supply comes from China. For a few specific items, like apple juice, garlic, canned mandarin oranges, fish, and shrimp, China is a major supplier. Imports from China accounted for about 60 percent of the U.S. apple juice supply and more than 50 percent of the garlic supply in 2007. Imports from China account for 10 percent of the U.S. shrimp supply, 2 percent of the catfish supply, and 8 percent of the basa (a type of catfish) supply. Basic foods that form the core of the U.S. diet—grain, meat, or dairy items—are generally not imported from China.

Data limitations constrain what is known about the safety of imported foods. ERS researchers analyzed FDA refusals of food import shipments originating from China by type of violation. Here, the term *violation* refers to products that appear to violate one or more of the laws enforced by FDA, such as those dealing with adulterated or misbranded products.

FDA refusals of food shipments from China peaked in early 2007, just before a series of highly publicized incidents. In 2007, FDA issued import alerts for wheat gluten, rice protein products, and five kinds of farm-raised fish and shrimp from China. Customs statistics show that shrimp imports from China slowed after the FDA alert was issued.

FDA refusals of Chinese food shipments reflect the mix of products imported: fish and shellfish, fruit, and vegetable products account for most refusals. Most Chinese food imports are processed to some degree, and the most common problems cited by FDA—"filth", unsafe additives, inadequate labeling, and lack of proper manufacturer registrations—are typically introduced during food processing and handling. Another of the most common problems—potentially harmful veterinary drug residues in farm-raised fish and shrimp—is introduced at the farm. FDA cites harmful pesticide residues and pathogens in Chinese food shipments less frequently.

Chinese authorities seek to control the safety of food exports by certifying exporters and the farms that supply them. Certified exporters constitute a small fraction of China's food industry. Most of China's 200 million farms and food companies are, in theory, excluded from export supply chains. Still, monitoring the wide range of products and hazards that can arise at varying points in the export supply chain is a challenge for Chinese and U.S. officials. Consultations and exchanges between Chinese and U.S. officials on food safety are an important step toward improving the effectiveness and efficiency of monitoring and enforcing U.S. food safety standards in food shipments from China to the United States. Safety-related measures, such as facilities upgrades, careful record-keeping, closer control over suppliers, testing, certifications, and audits, are likely to raise costs for Chinese food exporters.

How Was the Study Conducted?

ERS analyzed customs data on food imports from China to assess the trend and composition of imports. ERS obtained from FDA a comprehensive database on Import Refusal Reports (IRR) on Chinese food shipments refused entry into U.S. commerce between 1998 and 2004. ERS also downloaded more recent data for 2006-09 from the FDA web site. ERS tabulated the number of refusals of food shipments from China by year, product category, and violation in order to characterize the profile of potential safety problems in food imports. The FDA data reveal recurring problems in imported foods, but the data are not an indicator of the actual level or distribution of food safety risks that imports may pose to U.S. consumers. The study also describes recent developments in food safety monitoring and enforcement for Chinese food exports, certification of exporters, and consultations between U.S. and Chinese food safety officials.

Introduction

Rising consumption of imported foods poses challenges for U.S. food safety officials (Becker, 2008b; Buzby, 2003; Buzby et al., 2008). Retailers and processors seeking low-cost suppliers and exotic/ethnic foods demanded by U.S. consumers procure foods and ingredients all over the globe. It is often difficult to ensure that suppliers in far-flung locations operate according to the high safety standards and tight quality control demanded by U.S. consumers.

Recent incidents of food contamination and adulteration in Chinese food imports are a prominent manifestation of this issue. Adulterated milk, pet food, fish and shrimp, and news media reports about U.S. Food and Drug Administration (FDA) refusals of Chinese food shipments have created a groundswell of concern about the safety of food from China. Subsequent exchanges between U.S. and Chinese officials have addressed food safety issues. In 2007, a U.S. Interagency Working Group on Import Safety issued an *Action Plan for Import Safety* and FDA issued a *Food Protection Plan*.[1] FDA opened its first overseas office in China in 2008.

[1]See http://www.importsafety.gov/ and http://www.fda.gov/oc/initiatives/ advance/food/plan.html.

This report sets forth factual information about what foods the United States imports from China, safety risks that appear to be associated with those imports, and recent developments in food safety regulation and enforcement in China. The report provides a general assessment of where risks arise in the food supply chain. The analysis is based on customs statistics and data on FDA refusals of food shipments from China into the United States.

The processing, handling, and distribution of food in China is labor intensive.

Potential Safety Hazards

World attention was focused on Chinese food safety problems in 2008 when, by official accounts, six Chinese infants died and nearly 300,000 children were sickened with kidney ailments after consuming infant formula adulterated with melamine, an industrial chemical added to raw milk to raise its apparent protein content. China's top food safety official resigned, a company chairwoman and dozens of others were jailed, and other officials were fired. The problem spilled over into global markets when Chinese milk and other products (including candy, eggs, and biscuits) containing traces of melamine were found in other countries. The infant formula incident followed a string of domestic incidents, including an earlier series of infant deaths in 2004 from consuming fake milk powder; use of toxic dye in duck feed, chili sauce, and other foods; an outbreak of meningitis traced to snails served in a Beijing restaurant; periodic food poisonings in school or workplace cafeterias; use of industrial bleach to whiten noodles; carcinogenic drugs in fish and shrimp; poisoning from a steroid used in pork production; and the widespread sale of pork from pigs that were sick or had died from illness.[2]

Chinese food items have been periodically rejected in Japan, Europe, the United States, and elsewhere in recent years (Calvin et al.; Dong and Jensen). Japan introduced a stringent "positive list" system for testing food imports in 2006, largely in response to concerns about the quality of imports from China (Nelson and Sato). In early 2008, Japanese consumers were sickened by dumplings from China that were poisoned with pesticide residues, further elevating Japanese concerns about the safety of Chinese food imports. Inspections of imports from China by Thai health officials in 2007 found excessive pesticide residues in vegetables, high levels of sulfur dioxide in dried foods and preserves, and forbidden artificial colorings in candy (Ting).

In 2007, the United States encountered a series of widely publicized problems with Chinese imports. FDA issued import alerts after it detected melamine in wheat gluten and rice protein products and unsafe veterinary drug residues in five types of farm-raised fish and shrimp from China (Becker, 2008a; Schmit; Weise). In 2008, an import alert for milk products was issued in response to concerns about melamine adulteration. Since the 1980s, FDA's import alerts for Chinese products have also included red melon seeds (illegal dyes), bean curd (insect filth), dried fungus and mushrooms (filth from animals and insects), fresh garlic (mold, decomposition, insect filth/damage), and honey (fluoroquinolone residues) from China.

Potential food safety hazards in China stem from many sources. High crop yields and animal output from intensively cultivated land are achieved by widespread use of chemicals and veterinary drugs, some of which leave toxic residues on food. Banned toxic agricultural chemicals are still available through underground vendors. Even where they are not used, chemicals may still be present in the soil from use in past years or may drift when sprayed on adjacent fields. Many of China's farms and food processors are situated in heavily industrialized regions where water, air, and soil are contaminated by industrial effluents and vehicle exhaust. Hong Kong researchers found heightened levels of lead and cadmium in tests of crop soils from the Pearl River Delta region of southern China (Wong et al.). Contamination

[2]Schönmann describes a Chinese journalist's exposé on China's food safety problems. A Chinese language description of problems is offered by China Central Television.

from human and animal waste also contributes to poor water quality, partly because most rural areas lack sewage systems. It is common practice to let livestock and poultry roam freely in fields and to spread livestock and poultry waste on fields or use it as fish feed.

Many safety risks associated with foods imported from China are introduced in the manufacturing and handling of food. Poor handling and storage may introduce bacteria, viruses, parasites, fungi, and their toxins. Perishable vegetables and meat have traditionally been sold by small vendors the same day they are picked or slaughtered. Produce is typically transported in small open trucks. Refrigerated storage and transport equipment is relatively scarce. When temperature-controlled infrastructure is available, power outages, railroad delays, and differing temperature standards may lead to spoilage. Awareness of foodborne illness risks is relatively low in China, and the incidence of such illnesses reported by official statistics is probably underestimated (Wang and Ren; Schönmann). Many food processors use unsafe additives, toxic dyes, or fake ingredients to preserve food, cut production costs, or improve product appearance. The melamine-adulterated milk powder and pet food incidents brought attention to the widespread practice of adding melamine to feed and milk to artificially raise the apparent protein content. A presentation by officials overseeing food safety in the southern province of Guangdong cites a long list of problems found in food manufacturers, including outdated facilities with inadequate building materials, old rusty equipment, poor control of worker health and hygiene, weak monitoring of raw materials, contaminated water, and nonexistent or fraudulent recordkeeping (Zhang and Zhao). Food labels often lack proper descriptions of ingredients and nutritional information or are otherwise inadequate.

Making generalizations about China's food industry is difficult. Several thousand modern, large-scale, multinational and joint venture companies and farms that use best practices and sophisticated equipment operate alongside millions of small independent farms, workshops, and merchants that use crude equipment and techniques. China has some 200 million farming households with average land holdings of 1-2 acres per farm and at least 400,000 food processing enterprises, most with 10 or fewer employees. Millions of people and businesses are involved in the handling and transportation of food beyond the farm gate. The vast number of food suppliers increases the challenge of disseminating standards, monitoring production, and tracing problems to their source. In China's food sector, farmers and entrepreneurs frequently enter new industries and worker turnover is high. Consequently, many participants in food supply chains are unaware of standards and proper practices. Some producers and merchants in China's highly competitive market cut corners, add toxic substances, or skimp on safety controls to fatten razor-thin profit margins or gain some other competitive edge.

Chinese officials historically have been preoccupied with increasing the quantity of food to feed China's 1.3 billion people. Food safety became a government priority only during the first decade of the 21st century, when a series of action plans, regulations, and certification systems were enacted (see Cadilhon and Hoejskov; Calvin et al.; Ellis and Turner). Concerns about the use of unsafe pesticides, veterinary drugs, and rural pollution are so widespread that China's Ministry of Agriculture and Ministry of Environmental Protection have begun extensive national testing of vegetables, meat, and fish for chemical and drug residues and testing of rural soil, air, and water for heavy metals and other pollutants (Sun; Wu). National food safety standards and certification programs based on international standards have been put in place, but provinces and industries can set their own standards. The resulting array of differing standards creates confusion. Domestic food safety enforcement is mostly at the local level and can vary widely. Many local governments lack resources to enforce food safety. Local governments frequently have ties to industry that discourage tight regulatory oversight. Responsibility for regulating safety for exported food is concentrated in the national General Administration of Quality Supervision, Inspection, and Quarantine (AQSIQ) and its provincial branches. Food exporters commonly attain internationally recognized certifications, but producers of food for the domestic market are certified by local government organizations under domestic certification programs that are not well understood outside China.

A new Food Safety Law that took effect in June 2009 will attempt to address many of the long-recognized domestic food safety problems by establishing national food standards, setting up a food safety commission, requiring food manufacturers to keep extensive records, and making suppliers of food liable for food safety violations. However, the new law's effectiveness will depend on how it is implemented and enforced.

The general level of food safety in China seems to be improving, but it is difficult to assess the seriousness of problems or the degree of progress since information is closely guarded by the Chinese Government. For example, the Ministry of Agriculture's testing of vegetables, meats, and fish in domestic markets for pesticide and drug residues reported impressive compliance rates ranging from 91 to 100 percent in 2007. However, few details about the testing are made public, so the results are difficult to evaluate. China's Center for Disease Control and Prevention conducts extensive surveys of diet and nutrition that can trace intakes of toxic substances to types of food and regions, but these results are also not widely publicized (Ellis and Turner; Wu). Liaoning Province has a database of soil, water, and air pollution test results that identifies areas suitable for organic or "green" crops, but the information can be accessed only through government authorities (Gale, Avendaño, and Merel).

What Foods Are Imported From China?

The growing share of imported foods in U.S. supermarkets and restaurants presents new challenges for food safety regulators and private decision-makers (Becker, 2008b). While the U.S. food supply is still overwhelmingly from domestic sources, the share of imported foods has grown steadily (Jerardo). The growing presence of imported foods reflects various trends: seasonal demands for produce from warm-weather regions; rising consumer demand for ethnic food, beverages, and spices; integration of nontraditional regions into global supply chains; and falling agricultural trade barriers.

China is one of the most prominent examples of the emergence of a nontra-ditional supplier of food to the United States. Analysis of customs statistics shows that the annual value of food shipments from China rose from about $1 billion in 1999 to $5.2 billion in 2008 (fig. 1). Before 1999, the value of food imports from China was under $1 billion annually, and in 1999, China was the 11th-largest source of U.S. food imports. But in 2008, China was the third-largest supplier. The share of U.S. food imports (by value) coming from China rose from about 2 percent in the 1990s to 5.8 percent in 2008. The value of food imports from China was exceeded only by that of North American neighbors Canada and Mexico.[3]

[3]If the 27 European Union (EU) countries are counted as a single entity, imports from the EU also exceed imports from China.

The rise in food imports from China reflects robust demand for these prod-ucts as well as the eagerness of Chinese exporters to supply them. The growth coincides with China's December 2001 accession to the World Trade Organization, which not only lowered Chinese tariffs but also helped encourage a surge of Chinese food industry investment by both Chinese and multinational companies. Investment in China's food industry has been spurred by low labor costs and plentiful supplies of agricultural raw materials, like aquaculture products, fruits, and vegetables. Chinese prices of fish, fruit, and vegetables are as low as one-fifth to one-tenth of those in

Figure 1

Value of U.S. food imports from China, 1990-2008

$ billion

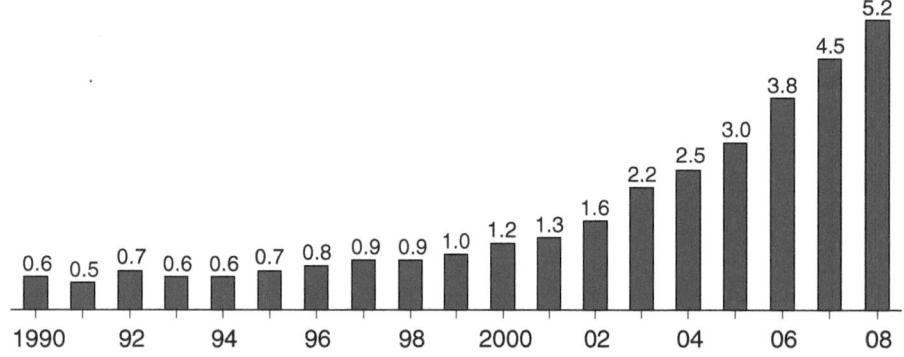

Note: The definition of food items used here includes edible plant and animal items, foods, beverages, and animal feeds. It excludes live animals, live plants, seeds, straw, hair, animal guts and bladders, waxes, fuel alcohol, and plants for medicinal uses. The definition includes Harmonized System codes 02, 03, 04, and 07-23, except for 1209, 1211, 1520, 1521, 1522, 2207.

Source: Estimated by ERS from U.S. Customs statistics accessed through Global Trade Information Services.

the United States (Gale and Tuan). Processing costs are so low that some fish, poultry, berries, and other products are imported to China, processed in factories along the Chinese coast, and re-exported (Sanchez, Franke, and Zecha). The Chinese Government supports agricultural and food exporters in various ways. Authorities give tax concessions, provide infrastructure and land, arrange low-interest bank loans, organize farmer supply chains, and assist exporters in obtaining required certifications and registrations (China Ministry of Foreign Trade and Commerce; Wang et al., 2009).

Food imports from China include a broad range of items, but about three-fourths fall into a few broad categories: fish and shellfish, juices, canned fruits, and other fruit, vegetable, and nut products. Nearly all imports are frozen, pickled, or further processed in factories along China's coast. Few unprocessed perishable foods are imported from China due to long distance and concerns about disease or pest transmission. Chinese meat and poultry have not been approved for import into the United States.[4] Bulk commodities (grains and oilseeds) are generally not imported from China. While China is now an important supplier of apple juice, garlic, canned mandarin oranges, fish, and shrimp consumed in the United States, imports from China account for less than 1 percent of the total U.S. food supply (see box, "Imports From China Account for a Small Share of the U.S. Food Supply").

Fish and shellfish (mostly frozen and prepared products) are the largest and fastest growing category of foods imported from China. In 2008, fish and shellfish imports accounted for 41 percent of the value of food imported from China (fig. 2). Fish and shellfish also accounted for 32 percent of the growth in Chinese food imports between 2002 and 2008 (table 1). Import volume exceeded 500,000 metric tons in 2008 (double the 2002 volume) and included tilapia, eels, cod, scallops, shrimp, prawns, crab, and various other fish.

[4]In 2006, USDA listed China as an eligible exporter of poultry, but Chinese exporters could only process and re-export poultry meat sourced in approved third countries. However, no eligible plants were approved, and subsequent legislation prevented implementation of the China approval. No trade has occurred to date.

Figure 2
Value of U.S. food imports from China by category, 2008

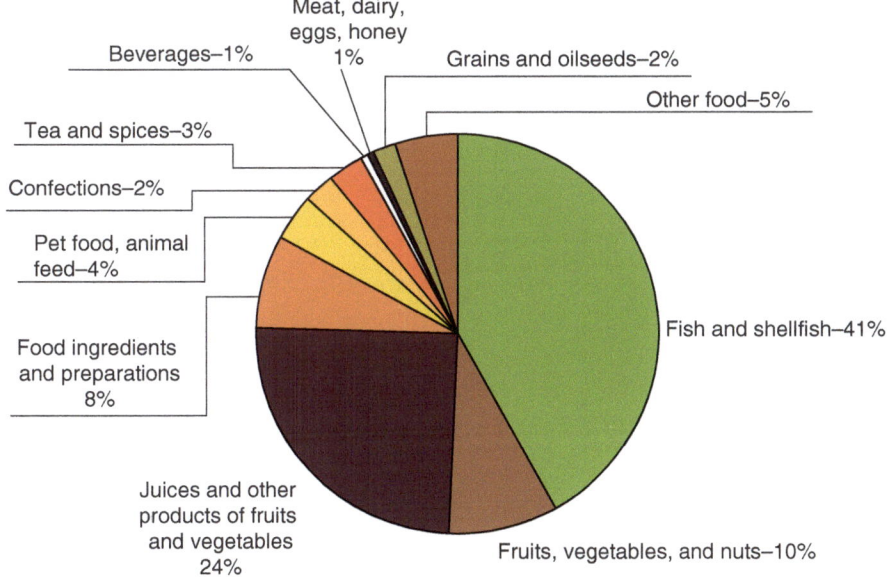

Note: Chart shows share of U.S. food imports from China by value. Percentages do not add to 100 due to rounding.

Source: ERS analysis of U.S. Customs statistics.

Imports From China Account for a Small Share of the U.S. Food Supply

Imports from China constitute a very small share of the total U.S. food supply. The most recent estimates show that imports from all countries together constituted about 7 percent of the U.S. food supply measured by value in 2005 (Jerardo).[1] Our tabulations of U.S. Customs statistics indicate that 5.8 percent of U.S. food imports (by value) came from China in 2008. Based on these figures, we estimate that food imports from China constituted approximately 0.4 percent of the U.S. food supply.

The role of imports from China in the U.S. food supply by value

Item	Share	Source
	Percent	
Food imports from all countries as a share of U.S. food supply, 2005	7.0	Jerardo[1]
Share of U.S. food imports that come from China, 2008	5.8	Calculated by authors from U.S. Customs statistics
Food imports from China as share of U.S. food supply	0.4	7%×5.8%

Source: Estimated from U.S. Department of Agriculture data.

Basic foods that form the core of the U.S. diet—grain, meat, or dairy items—are generally not imported from China. Grain and oilseed prices in China are generally higher than in the United States, so U.S. imports of Chinese grain are minimal. China exports very few dairy products to the United States. Imports of Chinese meat are also insignificant since China's meat- and poultry-processing plants have not been approved for export to the United States. The United States imports small quantities of rice and soybeans from China. Most of the rice is imported by Puerto Rico. Soybean imports from China are likely special varieties for direct human consumption or for use as organic animal feed.[2]

China is a major supplier of a few specific items, like apple juice, garlic, canned mandarin oranges, fish, and shrimp. Apple juice imports from China totaled 420 million gallons in 2007, which was 60 percent of the U.S. supply. Industry reports suggest that the share of garlic imported from China exceeded 50 percent in 2007 (Weise). FDA reported statistics provided by the National Oceanic and Atmospheric Administration that estimated imports from China account for 9.6 percent of the U.S. shrimp supply, 1.9 percent of the catfish supply, and 8 percent of the basa (a type of catfish) supply (U.S. Food and Drug Administration, 2007d).

---

[1]Jerardo reports that the imported share of food by volume is a higher value of 15 percent. Estimating the share of food imported from China by volume is difficult because consumption data are unavailable for many of the products imported. Chinese imports tend to be "high value" processed products like fish fillets and canned fruit rather than "low value" bulk products like grains, oilseeds, and unprocessed meats.

[2]U.S. soybean exports to China far exceed U.S. soybean imports from China.

Most of China's fish and shellfish products come from factories in coastal provinces that process fish and shellfish raised in ponds, lakes, or reservoirs tended by small-scale farmers. Chinese agricultural statistics indicate that fish and shellfish production doubled over the past decade; about two-thirds of production was cultivated, and a third was wild-caught (China National Bureau of Statistics, table 7-45). In addition, nearly 40 percent of exports are

Table 1
U.S. food imports from China by category

HS codes	Category *Main components*	2008 value	2002-08 growth
		Million $	
	All foods	5,162	3,531
03, 1605, 1606	Fish and shellfish *Tilapia, cod, scallops, shrimp, prawns, crab, and other fish*	2,162	1,148
07, 08, 20	Juices, fruit, vegetable, and nut products *Apple and pear juice, canned mandarins, fresh and dried garlic, canned and dried mushrooms, frozen vegetables, dried and canned beans*	1,732	1,365
11, 13, 15, 18, 1901, 21, 2301-2303	Food ingredients and preparations *Vegetable saps and extracts, cocoa butter, soy sauce, unspecified food preparations, malt extract, wheat gluten, and starch*	394	276
2309	Pet food and animal feed *Pet snacks and food*	193	169
17	Candy and confections	126	80
09	Tea and spices *Tea leaves, chili powder/paste, ginger*	407	252
0409	Honey	6	-2
22	Beverages *Sweetened water, beer, ethyl alcohol, vinegar*	30	16
02, 04 (except 0409), 1602, 1603	Meat and dairy *Frog legs, rabbit*	26	11
10,12	Grains and oilseeds *Rice, soybeans*	94	88
	Other foods	257	141

Note: HS refers to harmonized system of codes for classifying products in international trade statistics. "Food" is as defined in figure 1.

Source: ERS analysis of U.S. Customs data accessed through Global Trade Information Services.

produced from imported fish and shellfish that are processed in China and re-exported (China Food Industry Net). Sanchez, Franke, and Zecha estimate that most U.S. seafood exports to China are re-exported.

Fruits, vegetables, nuts, juices and other fruit and vegetable products account for about a third of the value of U.S. food imports from China. The total for this broad category was $1.7 billion in 2008, over four times the value in 2002. Most of these products are processed; relatively few fresh produce items are imported from China. Perishable items are hard to keep fresh over long shipping distances, and U.S. regulations forbid import of some kinds of Chinese fresh produce due to concerns about potential disease and pest contamination. Moreover, processing costs are low in China. The largest component of this category is fruit juice (mainly apple juice), accounting for $677 million in 2008.[5] Vegetable imports totaled $282 million. Fresh and chilled garlic and onions (the most prominent unprocessed vegetable

[5]China is a major exporter of apples to other countries, but Chinese apples are not allowed to be imported to the United States due to phytosanitary concerns.

Fish are often raised in ponds where they feed on waste from poultry and livestock.

items) accounted for about $70 million (75,000 metric tons), and dried and powdered garlic imports accounted for another $36 million (50,000 metric tons). Mushrooms and fungi ($110 million)—most in canned, preserved, processed, or dried form—are another important vegetable import category. Other vegetables imported from China include dried and canned black and kidney beans, peas, peppers, and vegetables, like pickled radish, bamboo shoots, water chestnuts, and napa cabbage used in Chinese cuisine. Nut imports, mainly pine and macadamia nuts, totaled $80 million.

The remaining one-fourth of food imports from China includes a wide array of items, like tea, noodles, and vegetable saps and extracts (most of which appear to have nonfood uses[6]), ginseng, pastries, baked goods, soy sauce, tofu, beer, and liquor. Many of these items are Chinese specialty foods, like Chinese brands of beer and liquor, Chinese-style snacks, and cooking ingredients, that are likely sold through Asian specialty stores or restaurants. Some are used in Chinese traditional medicines or consumed as nutritional supplements.

[6]Vegetable sap and extract imports from China are split between two categories—"substances having anaesthetic, prophylactic, or therapeutic properties" (HS1302194040) and "other vegetable saps and extracts" (HS1302194090).

China is also emerging as a source of ingredients used in food processing. Imports of miscellaneous food preparations, malt extract, and protein concentrates are small in quantity but could pose a food safety risk if products are adulterated. Wheat gluten is a relatively minor food import, but a major incident resulted when its adulteration with the toxic chemical melamine in 2007 was linked to pet deaths in the United States. Wheat gluten imports more than doubled in 2006 to just under $20 million but fell to less than $6 million in 2008 after FDA issued an import alert for Chinese wheat gluten in 2007. Pet food and animal feed imports from China totaled $193 million in 2008, which consisted of $131 million in pet food and over $50 million in poultry feed, additives, and other feeds.

FDA Refusals of Imports From China

ERS analyzed data on FDA import refusals of food shipments in order to characterize the types of problems that occur in food imports from China. FDA can refuse food imports that appear to be adulterated, misbranded, or fail to comply with U.S. labeling requirements or other laws. (USDA's Food Safety and Inspection Service is responsible for meat and poultry imports, but as previously mentioned, Chinese meat and poultry products are not currently exported to the United States.) We first analyzed reports of "entry lines" (unique shipments or lots of products or items offered for admission into U.S. commerce) that were refused entry into the United States by FDA between 1998 and 2004 (Buzby et al., 2008). We supplemented that data with more recent reports of refusals of shipments from China between 2006 and 2009 obtained from the FDA web site.

FDA refusals are a general indicator of the frequency and type of recurring problems that appear in food shipments. The refusal reports are administrative records; they are not intended to be a statistical indicator of food safety problems, so the data should be interpreted carefully (see box, "FDA Import Refusal Data", p.12). FDA inspects less than 1 percent of food shipments destined for the United States, and it performs laboratory examinations on an even smaller percentage of shipments.[7] The refusal data do not include consistent measures of the value or volume of an entry line so we cannot calculate the value or share of food imports refused.

Becker's (2008b) analysis of FDA refusals for fiscal year (FY) 2007 (October 2006-September 2007) showed that China's share of import refusals that year—8.6 percent—was more than twice its 3.3-percent share of entry lines handled by FDA.[8] The figures reported by Becker imply that 0.27 percent of entry lines from China was refused, higher than the 0.1 percent for all entry lines. Although these figures indicate that China accounts for a disproportionately large share of refusals, as Becker notes, we cannot draw strong conclusions from these figures about the safety of imports from China.

China's State Council reported a 0.8-percent rejection rate for food shipments to the United States in 2006, a figure cited by Chinese officials as evidence that the country's food exports are overwhelmingly safe. However, this statistic hides higher refusal rates for certain products. For example, FDA reports that its tests of fish and shrimp during October 2006-May 2007 found excessive drug residues in 22 of 89 samples of fish and shrimp, a rejection rate of 25 percent (U.S. Food and Drug Administration, 2007a). Also in 2007, FDA reported that 44 percent of wheat gluten samples and 32 percent of rice protein concentrate samples tested positive for melamine. All of the positive samples were traced to China (U.S. Food and Drug Administration, 2007b).

Our tabulation of monthly FDA refusals of entry lines from China from June 2006 to February 2009 shows surges of refusals during the early months of 2007 and in January 2009 (fig. 3).[9] The number of refusals was 80 or higher in 6 of 7 months from December 2006 to June 2007, peaking at about 150 in April 2007 and 140 in January 2009. The average number of refusals over the entire June 2006-February 2009 period was 69 per month.

[7]Food and Water Watch reported that less than 2 percent of fish and seafood shipments were inspected by FDA in 2003-06.

[8]China's share of entry lines (3.3 percent) is less than its share of the value of U.S. food imports (5.8 percent) that we calculated from Customs statistics. We found that China was the third-largest source of food imports by value, but it was only the sixth-largest source of entry lines handled by FDA.

[9]The 2006-09 data were acquired from the FDA web site, which posts data for 12 months at a time. We began collecting the data in May 2007 and were able to obtain data beginning from June 2006. The 1998-2004 database was obtained through an interagency agreement (Buzby et al., 2008).

The 2007 surge preceded the series of incidents that generated wide publicity that year. In July and August 2007, FDA issued import alerts for wheat gluten and rice protein (following the detection of melamine) and five kinds of fish and shrimp (following the detection of unsafe levels of toxic veterinary drug residues) from China. The Janury 2009 peak in refusals followed an FDA alert issued in November 2008 for products from China containing milk due to concerns about melamine adulteration. Over 70 shipments of candy, cocoa mixes, cookies, and pet snacks were refused for melamine adulteration during January 2009, up from 7 in December 2008. Melamine was cited in 41 refusals during February 2009.

Analysis of the FDA data for 1998-2009 suggests that the surge in early 2007 was unusual. The more than 1,000 refusals of Chinese products during 2007 was about 50 percent greater than the 600-700 annual refusals during calendar years 2002-04 (fig. 4). There were unusually few refusals during 1999-2001—about 150-300 per year versus about 490 in 1998—but this pattern followed a general one of lower refusals from all countries during

Figure 3

Monthly FDA import refusals of food shipments from China

Number

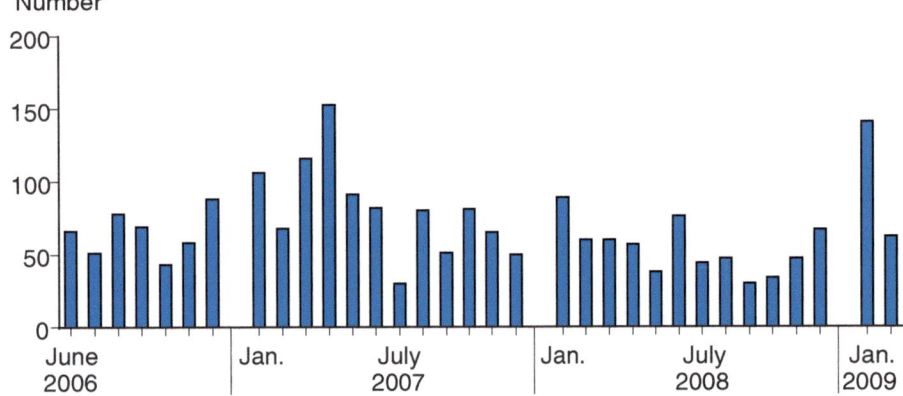

Source: ERS analysis of U.S. Food and Drug Administration import refusal data.

Figure 4

FDA refusals of food entry lines from China, 1998-2008

Number

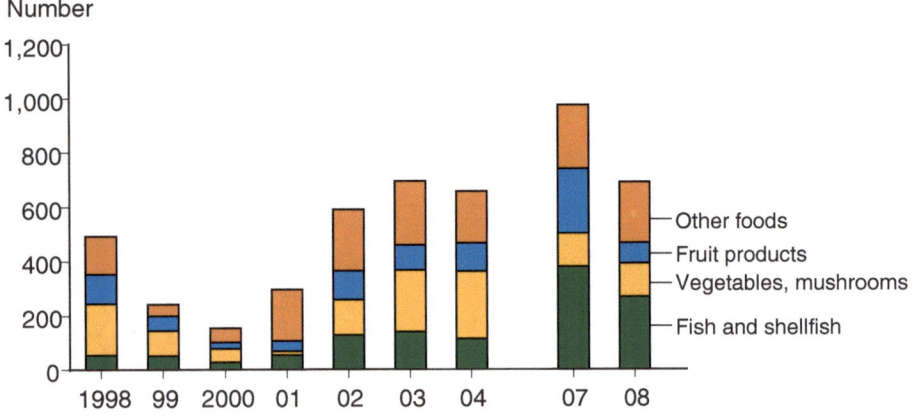

Note: Data are for calendar years. Data were not available for January 2005-May 2006.

Source: ERS analysis of U.S. Food and Drug Administration import refusal data.

FDA Import Refusal Data

FDA generates computerized Import Refusal Reports that record the product, its supplier, country of origin, and the reason(s) that products are refused entry into U.S. commerce (U.S. Food and Drug Administration, 2004). Imported food must be free from adulteration, be properly and truthfully labeled in English, and comply with all other U.S. laws and standards. Buzby et al. (2008) and Becker (2008b) provide greater detail on FDA's import program and the FDA data.

The FDA data must be interpreted carefully since they are not a representative sample of all food imports. The data reveal recurring problems that appear in imported foods, but they do not indicate the actual level or distribution of food safety risk that imports may pose to U.S. consumers. FDA inspects a small proportion of food import shipments. Shipments are targeted for inspection or other administrative actions to assess existing and emerging problems identified by FDA. Thus, the pattern of refusals may reflect where FDA has focused its import alerts and monitoring efforts.

Note that *violations* cited in import refusals refer to products that *appear* to be adulterated, misbranded, or in violation of laws enforced by FDA. According to England (2000) of FDA, "the significance of the appearance standard under U.S. law is that the Government is NOT required to prove an actual violation of law or the regulations has occurred. Rather, FDA must be able to show that there exists an "appearance" of a violation to refuse admission of goods."

FDA reports are based on "entry lines"—individual, unique lots of a particular food offered for import into U.S. commerce by a particular importer/producer at a particular point in time. When FDA refuses an item, it assigns violation codes to document the reasons for the refusal (see http://www.fda.gov/ora/oasis/ora_oasis_viol_rpt.html). Multiple violations can be associated with a refusal of a particular entry line.

The number of refusals posted on the FDA web site (www.fda.gov/ora/oasis/ora_ref_cntry.html) includes many nonfood shipments because FDA also oversees imports of pharmaceuticals, medical devices, and radiation-emitting equipment. We deleted records with product descriptions that indicated the shipment contained nonfood items. For August 2008, for example, the FDA site shows 146 refusals for China, but 100 of those were nonfood entry lines, such as medical equipment, cosmetics, televisions, toothbrushes, and nutritional supplements.

The 1998-2004 data included detailed information on refusals, but the newer data from the FDA web site included only the product name, supplier name and location, and violation codes. The data for 1998-2004 include three types of product descriptions describing the shipment, but the more recent 2006-08 data only include a less structured product description provided by the importer on the shipment invoice.

that period observed by Buzby et al. (2008, p. 7). The 690 refusals during 2008 were comparable to the number of refusals during 2003-04. Refusals of fish and shellfish products were higher during 2007-08 than in earlier years. Refusals of fruit products surged in 2007 before falling in 2008. Refusals of vegetable products during 2007-08 were fewer than in previous years.

The number of refusals from China has not grown nearly as fast as the growth of food imports from China noted above. The increase in FDA refusals may have been constrained by FDA's limited resources. The number of food entry lines under FDA's responsibility tripled between FY 1997 and FY 2007, and the percentage of shipments inspected has reportedly fallen from 8 percent in 1992 to 1 percent in recent years (Becker, 2008b; Schmit). Changes in refusals could also stem from differences in reporting procedures or from the increased number of inspections (Buzby et al.).

Three Industry Categories Account for Most Refusals

Analysis of refusals by industry group shows that three broad categories of products—fish and shellfish, fruit products, and vegetable products—combined accounted for 70 to 80 percent of FDA import refusals from China in recent years (fig. 5). Whereas, in 2002-04, these three categories accounted for about half of refusals for all countries.

Fish and shellfish products were the industry group with the most refusals from China, followed by vegetables and fruit products. Fish/shellfish share of refusals from China doubled from about 20 percent in 2000-04 to nearly 40 percent in 2007-08. Buzby et al. found that fish/shellfish and vegetable products had the largest share of refusals from all countries, with about 20 percent each. Becker (2008b) reached a similar conclusion in analysis of 2006/07 data. Food and Water Watch also drew attention to the high incidence of safety problems with fish and shellfish imports from China.

Eels (frozen and/or roasted), catfish fillets, and shrimp accounted for most of the refused fish/shellfish shipments, but a wide variety of other products were also refused, including tilapia, tuna, monk fish, squid, jellyfish, crawfish, crab, cod, mackerel, and other fish species. Most of these products were processed in some manner—frozen, breaded, filleted, de-boned, and/or skinless. The large number of fish and shellfish refusals may reflect increased monitoring of these products that began in 2006 due to chronic problems

Figure 5

Share of FDA refusals by industry

Percent

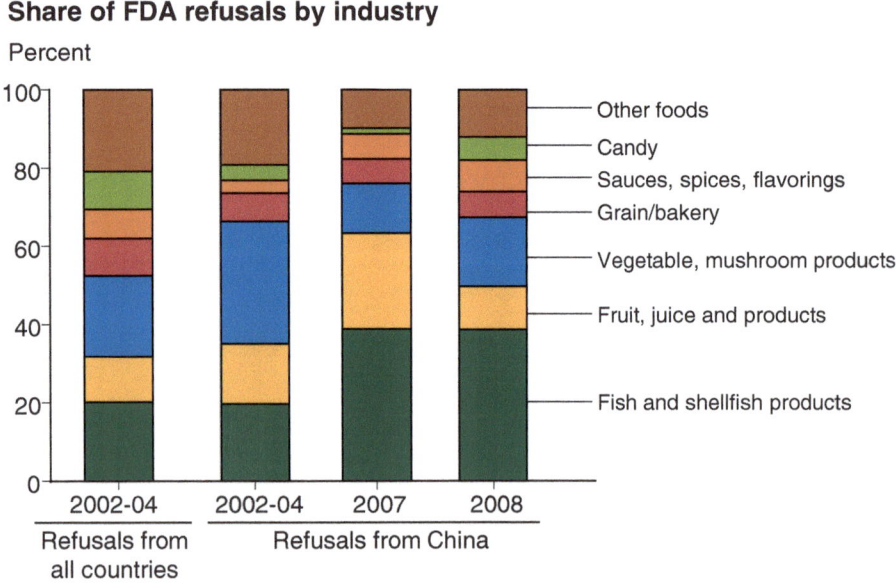

Source: ERS analysis of FDA import refusal data and Buzby et al.

with veterinary drug residues and unsafe additives in aquaculture products. Schmit reported that FDA devoted half of its testing of aquaculture products to shipments from China due to widespread problems. In 2006, FDA issued an import alert for eels produced in China, and on June 28, 2007, an alert was issued for all farm-raised catfish, basa (a type of catfish), shrimp, dace (related to carp), and eel from China (Kraemer; see box, "Import Alert Slows Shrimp Imports"). While the alert is in effect, these products are refused unless they can be shown to be free of harmful drug residues. Many of the import refusals were eels and shrimp covered by this alert.

Refused fruit product shipments included mainly preserved, dried, and salted plums, haw (similar to crab apple), goji berries, wolfberries, several other types of dried or preserved fruits, and some fruit drinks. Vegetable products were the leading refusal category in 2002-04, but the number was markedly lower in 2007-08.

It is not clear whether the reduced refusals of vegetable products reflected an improvement in compliance for these products or whether some other factor was responsible. Most vegetable refusals appeared to be products used in Asian cuisine. Mushroom and fungus products (dried, boiled, and canned) were the predominant vegetable type refused. Others frequently refused included bamboo shoots, ginger, and pickled radish and cabbage. Nearly all vegetable and fruit product refusals were processed to some extent.

Many of the other refusals from China during 2007-08 appeared to be distinctively Asian products. Tofu and soy sauce accounted for most of the refusals under sauces/special foods, and soybeans accounted for many of the refusals in the nuts and edible seed category. One type of non-Asian food with multiple refusals was candy, including bubble gum, candy canes, chewy candy, and chocolate. In past years, candy accounted for a relatively small share of refusals from China, but refusals in this category rose in 2008. Grain and bakery products (including noodles and almond cookies) also accounted for a relatively small share of Chinese refusals. Among the "Other food" category, common refusals included tea-based drinks and pet snacks.

Another notable result is the absence of several large import items from the refusal list during 2007-08. Several of the largest food import categories—garlic, apple juice, and honey—had only a handful of FDA refusals during this period.

Most Common Violations

FDA has cited over 50 different violations in its refusals of Chinese products, but most fall into a few general categories that include general filth, unsafe additives or chemicals, microbial contamination, inadequate labeling, and lack of proper manufacturer registrations.[10] Here, we analyzed the FDA data on refusals of Chinese food imports by violation for 2002-04 and 2007-08 to characterize the types of problems occurring in imports from China (fig. 6).[11] Our tabulations show the most frequently occurring violations in Chinese shipments. The occurrence of violations in products from all countries for 2002-04 is shown for comparison. Note that this analysis is based on the total number of violations and that many refusals had multiple violations. For example, many fish refusal reports listed both veterinary drug residues and filth violations; each of these violations were counted separately in this part of the analysis.[12]

[10]Keep in mind that FDA can refuse products based on the appearance of a violation, so these refusals are in fact based on "apparent violations," but we drop the "apparent" in this discussion to avoid repetition and enhance readability.

[11]We combined data for 2007-08 in this analysis since the pattern of violations in the 2 years was similar.

[12]Buzby et al. found the average number of violations per shipment to be between 1.3 and 2.0 for various industry groups.

Import Alert Slows Shrimp Imports

FDA issues import alerts on products and shippers that have food safety or other problems in violation of the laws enforced by the agency. Alerts can apply to all shipments of a particular product from a country or from specific firms. Firms can have their products exempt if they demonstrate to FDA that they have adequate internal quality controls and processes in place and can document a history of problem-free shipments.

In 2007, FDA issued import alert no. 16-131 for four kinds of farm-raised fish—catfish, basa, dace (related to carp), and eel—and shrimp from anywhere in China. The alert was triggered by chronic problems with drug residues in imported fish and shrimp and was the latest in a series of related alerts issued since 2001 (Acheson; Kraemer). During increased monitoring of these products from October 1, 2006, through May 31, 2007, FDA found drug residues in 25 percent of the samples it tested. The main residues detected included malachite green, nitrofurans, and gentian violet (banned in the United States as potential carcinogens) and fluoroquinolones (banned in the United States due to concerns that ingestion by humans might build up antibiotic resistance). Malachite green and nitrofurans were also banned in China in 2002, but FDA continued to detect residues in some imports from China. Fluoroquinolones are permitted for use in China.

Shipments covered by the alert can be released into U.S. commerce if third-party test results or other evidence is provided to prove that the product is free of harmful drug residues. By April 2008, FDA had detained nearly 3,000 shipments and 1,387 had been released into U.S. commerce following laboratory tests (Kraemer). In 2008, FDA and Chinese authorities formed a working group to focus on improving aquatic products' safety (U.S. Food and Drug Administration, 2007d).

Analysis of customs statistics suggests that the import alert slowed a surge of shrimp imports. U.S. imports of processed shrimp (HS code 160520) from China were unusually high during the months preceding the alert. Imports were 6,000-7,000 metric tons (mt) monthly from September 2006 to January 2007 before falling off according to seasonal patterns (see figure below). Following the alert announced June 28, 2007, imports slowed but did not cease entirely. Imports slowed to 2,000 mt or less for July-October 2007 and slowed further in 2008. Shrimp imports for 2008 averaged 2,600 mt monthly in 2008, down from over 4,800 mt in 2006. FDA import refusals of entry lines from China due to veterinary drug residues averaged about 15 per month in the 12 months after the import alert, almost identical to the average during the 12-month period before the alert.

Monthly U.S. processed shrimp imports from China, 2006-08

1,000 metric tons

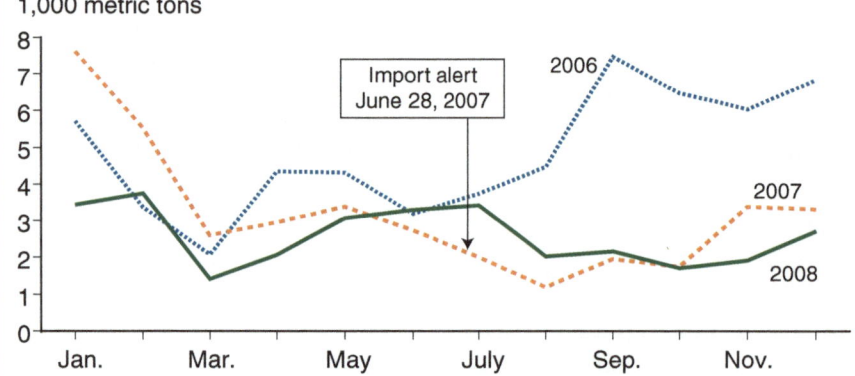

Note: Figure shows monthly U.S. imports (HS code 160520) from China.
Source: ERS analysis of U.S. Customs data accessed through Global Trade Information Services.

Figure 6

Violations cited in FDA refusals of food imports from China[1]

Percent

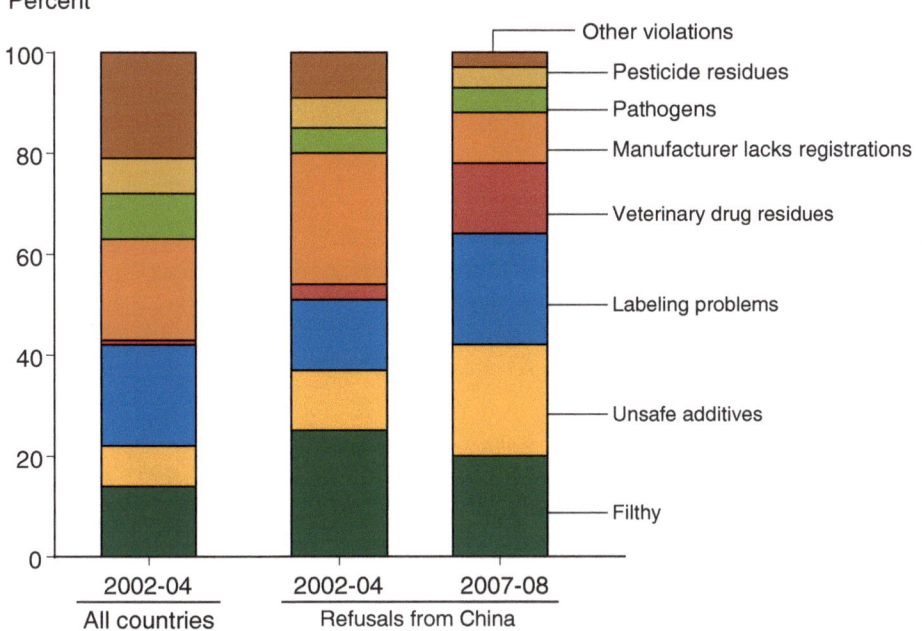

Note: Chart shows share of violations in FDA import refusal reports. Many refused shipments had multiple violations.

[1]For a description of violation codes, see http://www.fda.gov/ora/oasis/ora_oasis_viol_rpt.html.

Source: ERS analysis of FDA import refusal reports.

The most common violations during 2007-08 included "filthy" and unsafe additives, each of which accounted for 20 percent of violations. These violations together accounted for 42 percent of violations for China shipments, nearly double the share of violations from all countries (a combined 22 percent). "Filthy" violations occurred when the food appeared to contain a filthy, putrid, or decomposed substance (like human or animal hair, feces, insects, or dirt), was spoiled, or was otherwise unfit for food (20 percent of violations for 2007-08 and 25 percent for 2002-04). This category also included some shipments rejected for containing non-nutritional substances or embedded foreign objects. Filthy violations occurred frequently for all types of products. Unsafe additives, including colorings or dyes, dulcin, cyclamate, and excess sulfite levels, accounted for 22 percent of 2007-08 violations. Melamine adulteration is included in this category. Unsafe additives were most common in fruit products. The unsafe additive share of violations in shipments from China is much higher than the share among shipments from all countries.

Labeling problems accounted for about 22 percent of 2007-08 violations. Labeling problems included lack of clear English labeling that truthfully identified ingredients, weight or count, nutritional information, and whether the food contained artificial coloring or sweeteners. Manufacturers' lack of proper registration (for example, when a manufacturer of low-acid canned food or acidified food failed to file information on its scheduled process or register its plant with FDA) accounted for about 10 percent of China shipment violations during 2007-08. This violation was most common for vegetable products, most of which are pickled, dried, or otherwise processed.

The most recent period had a high incidence of veterinary drug residue problems that were likely linked to FDA's more careful examination of fish and seafood during that period. Veterinary drug residues are a common problem in fish and shrimp shipments and were the fourth most frequent category of problems overall during 2007-08, accounting for 14 percent of violations. Most fish and shrimp imported from China are cultured in ponds that frequently have poor water quality. Farmers commonly use drugs to control disease and fungal infections in these ponds. Veterinary drug residues can also be a problem in other farm animals and their products, such as bees and honey. The type of drug residue is not usually reported by FDA, but some shipments of honey were found to contain chloramphenicol, an antibiotic that is a known carcinogen and has also been linked to aplastic anemia, a rare and generally fatal side effect in humans. Nearly all veterinary drug residue violations were in fish and shrimp products (the United States does not import meat or poultry from China).

Other types of adulteration included unsafe pesticide residues, pathogens, and pathogen toxins. Pathogens appear to be a problem mainly in fish and seafood shipments. *Salmonella* was found mainly in fish, seafood, spices, and flavorings, and *Listeria* was found in fish and seafood. Other bacteria were found on a variety of products. Aflatoxin, a carcinogenic byproduct of mold infestations in food crops, was found on nuts, seeds, and candy (which may contain nuts). Pesticide residues were a less frequently occurring problem during 2007-08, accounting for about 4 percent of violations, down from 6 percent during 2002-04. Unsafe pesticide residues were found on some vegetables and their products: celery, soybeans, lotus, pea pods, mushrooms, scallions, ginger, and ginseng. Several shipments of purportedly organic beans and berries were refused for unsafe pesticide residues. A number of shipments of eels were also contaminated with pesticides.[13]

[13]A China Central Television investigative report discovered an individual who sprayed pesticide on drying fish to keep insects away. Eels may have been contaminated with pesticides by this practice.

Most of the violations flagged by FDA in imports from China over the analyzed periods were problems linked to the processing and handling of food products rather than to farm production practices. Filth generally results from introducing dirt or foreign materials in unsanitary packing or processing facilities. Unsafe additives are generally added by processors to enhance color or flavor or to preserve products. Unsafe additives are a much more common violation among Chinese refusals than those for all countries, and the share of unsafe additive violations increased between 2002-04 and 2007-08.

Lack of English-language labels that clearly describe ingredients is typically the responsibility of the manufacturer or packer. Labeling was one of the most common problems among Chinese violations (22 percent during 2007-08 and 14 percent during 2002-04), as it was among shipments from all countries (20 percent during 2002-04). The share of Chinese violations due to manufacturer registration problems declined from 26 percent in 2002-04 to 10 percent in 2007-08, perhaps reflecting Chinese regulators' emphasis on ensuring that exporters have proper registrations and certifications (described below).

Farm-level problems were cited less frequently. One farm-level problem—veterinary drug residues in fish and shrimp—stands out with 14 percent of violations during 2007-08, up from 4 percent of violations during 2002-04. FDA has been concerned about veterinary drug residue problems in Chinese fish and shrimp for some time (Kraemer), but the recent high incidence of

This extension station sells seeds and other farm inputs, but many Chinese farmers purchase from unlicensed dealers who sell poor quality seeds and toxic chemicals.

veterinary drug violations may reflect the 2007 FDA import alert for this issue. Unsafe pesticide residues, which stem mostly from farm production practices and environmental conditions, also accounted for just 4 percent of violations.

Farm-level problems like unsafe pesticide residues and heavy metal contamination could be more prevalent than indicated by FDA violations. Toxic residues can be detected only through lab tests, so they could be present in untested shipments that are rejected for more obvious violations, such as filth and inadequate labeling. Pesticide residues and heavy metal contaminants have been a major concern in China's exports to Japan and Hong Kong and in produce sold in China's domestic market. Likewise, pathogen problems account for a small percentage of violations identified by FDA refusals, but these are potentially serious because pathogens may lead to acute and chronic illness and premature death. Domestic pathogen-related food poisonings, usually linked to school or workplace cafeterias, are a common problem in China (Wang et al., 2007).

Efforts To Improve Chinese Food Safety

U.S. and Chinese officials are involved in complex multi-pronged efforts to address potential safety risks from food imports from China. These efforts include inspecting and testing products at the border as well as measures to address hazards at their source in processing plants and on farms, an approach stressed by the U.S. Interagency Working Group on Import Safety, U.S. Congress, and FDA's *Action Plan for Import Safety* (Becker, 2008a).

China's Food Safety System

Since 2002, Chinese authorities have been attacking food safety problems at all points in the supply chain (China State Council). They have stepped up regulation and enforcement for both domestic and exported food, but safety standards for exports are generally higher and more stringently enforced than those for domestic food (Calvin et al.; Dong and Jensen). Domestic food safety responsibilities are split among provincial and city agricultural, commerce, technical supervision, and health bureaus (see Ellis and Turner, pp. 43-44). Export food safety is centralized in the ministry-level General Administration of Quality Supervision, Inspection, and Quarantine (AQSIQ) and its provincial branches—known as CIQs—which are directly under AQSIQ's authority. AQSIQ requires that exported food meet domestic Chinese standards as well as those of the importing company and country. The CIQ tests product samples at the point of export to ensure compliance with safety standards. Beginning September 2007, each exported shipment inspected by entry-exit or quarantine authorities was required to have a seal from AQSIQ.

Domestic food safety efforts tend to lag behind those directed at exports. Chinese officials—in response to both domestic and international safety incidents—have stepped up domestic inspection and testing of food, introduction and dissemination of standards, and regulation of food producers and have initiated other measures aimed at achieving a broad-based improvement in the general level of food safety. Some of the prominent measures include the following (Calvin et al.; Ellis and Turner; Cadilhon and Hoejskov):

- Restricting agricultural production to areas free of contamination by heavy metals, like lead, cadmium, mercury, and arsenic, and controlling use of dangerous chemicals in agricultural production.

- Inspecting and testing final products in domestic wholesale and retail markets for compliance with chemical residue standards.

- Constructing a vast network of government laboratories to test agricultural products, soil, air, and water in rural areas.

- Setting up hundreds of central and provincial government demonstration projects related to "safe" agriculture.

- Implementing domestic certification programs (some voluntary, some mandatory) for food manufacturers and farms.

- Linking "production bases" (company farms or groups of small farmers) with processors or packing houses to standardize agricultural products and to control use of chemicals and veterinary drugs.

- Setting up a product tracking and tracing system.

- Publishing a "blacklist" of banned food additives.

Approved Exporters

China's approach to export food safety emphasizes creation of closed supply chains limited to elite export-oriented companies and farms that can demonstrate that they have instituted appropriate safety controls and have high sanitation standards, qualified personnel, and control over raw materials to ensure safety of their products. AQSIQ requires that exporting companies apply to their provincial CIQ for a sanitation registration. The company provides information on the production facility, equipment, its products, countries to which it exports, water quality and treatment, production process, worker qualifications, laboratory equipment, raw material sources, and certifications it has obtained. Exporters of most food products must procure agricultural raw materials from a registered "production base"—a farm controlled by the company directly or a fixed group of farm suppliers that supply the company with raw materials.[14] In order to facilitate "trace back" capability, AQSIQ requires exporters to keep production records on their source of raw materials. Producers of raw materials are required to keep records of where products were grown, dates of planting and harvesting, and chemical applications. An inspection by CIQ auditors determines whether the company can be certified.[15] The closed supply chain approach is illustrated by China's agreement with Hong Kong, which restricts exports to a limited number of Chinese suppliers. Shipments must be accompanied by a health/sanitation certificate and are restricted to certain border crossings where compulsory checks are performed (Thompson; Sanchez, Franke, and Zecha). In theory, the registration system limits the pool of exporters to an elite minority of suppliers. According to a 2007 report by China's State Council, only about 12,000 of 448,000 food processing enterprises in China were approved to export food, and only 380,000 hectares out of 121 million hectares of farmland were of suppliers approved for growing export crops.

Lists of approved exporters of selected products to specific countries are posted on the AQSIQ web site (http://english.aqsiq.gov.cn/SpecialTopics/ ImportandExportFoodSafety/DataService/). Some provincial CIQ web sites include subsets of the national lists showing exporters from their province, but we did not find a master list of all registered exporters. When ERS checked the site in March 2009, the English-language section contained lists of about 90 companies approved to export aquatic products, 190 companies approved to export poultry and eggs, and over 800 fruit packing houses registered to export. The site listed companies approved to export vegetables, pork, honey, and ginger to Hong Kong, Macao, and Japan. Most of these companies are not eligible to export to the United States because China does not currently export meat, poultry, or apples to the United States. The lists included company name, location, the name and area of the farms supplying the company, the provincial CIQ office responsible for that company, and the countries to which the company exports.

In theory, restricting imports to suppliers within the AQSIQ system may improve food safety. However, considerable resources will be required to continually monitor so many companies and production bases and keep the

[14]The Shandong CIQ requires exported spinach and other exported crops considered vulnerable to safety problems to be grown on land controlled directly by the exporting company.

[15]During interviews in 2007, representatives of the Liaoning CIQ said that over 50 percent of applicants pass the initial inspection, about 40 percent are required to make improvements, and 1-2 percent are refused. The CIQ certification must be renewed after 3 years (Gale, Avendaño, and Merel).

information up to date. A journalists' investigation of the export registration in Shaanxi Province noted that some exporters' monitoring of raw material sources had not kept pace with their upgrade of facilities and expanded scale of operations (Yang). Exporter lists on the AQSIQ site were about 2 years old when ERS checked them in March 2009. The AQSIQ site listed over 1,000 export-approved aquaculture "production bases" controlled by nearly 400 companies and nearly 400 poultry production bases controlled by 90 companies. While these are a small percentage of all producers in China, regular inspections and audits of this many companies and farms would require substantial human and financial resources. Other difficulties include changes of name and/or location, varying English translations of Chinese company names, and multiple companies with the same owner (see box, "Profile of a Chinese Fish Exporter"). Some lists were translated into English, but much of the material is published only in Chinese.

To investigate potential problems, ERS cross-checked FDA refusal reports with the list of aquatic product exporters. FDA's import refusal reports for August 2008 listed refusals of shrimp at ports in Florida, Los Angeles, and New York from two Chinese companies in the city of Zhanjiang in Guangdong Province. Neither of these companies was on the list of approved aquatic product exporters, although the list included dozens of companies in the same city. The web site of one of the companies with rejected shrimp (http://www.zjlw.com.cn) notes that the founder owns five seafood companies with distinctly different names.[16] A company with products placed on an alert potentially could ship the same products under the name of a related company.

[16]None of these company names were found on the AQSIQ exporter list or in FDA refusal reports, but one company was found on a Canadian import refusal report.

AQSIQ uses inducements and punishments to enforce export safety. Companies and CIQ officials that approve shipments are subject to fines for shipments that fail to pass inspections in importing countries. AQSIQ established lists of "famous brand" and "inspection-exempt" food exporters. The domestic "inspection-exempt" program was abandoned in September 2008 when milk sold by companies on the list was found to be adulterated with melamine. In addition, a "blacklist" of companies with a history of violations is banned from exporting (http://www.aqsiq.gov.cn/ztlm/jckspwgqymd/). The February 2009 blacklist included 105 companies (up from 66 on the December 2007 list), about half of them identified as exporting to the United States.[17] Fish and eel were the most common products of blacklist companies, but many companies selling vegetable and fruit products were also listed.[18] Seventy-three blacklist companies were cited for "evading inspection and quarantine." Other violations included excessive drug and pesticide residues; falsified documents; lack of registration in the importing country, including products from outside the authorized export base; and switching substandard products for compliant ones. An AQSIQ investigation of Chinese firms placed on FDA import alert in 2007 concluded that the alerts resulted from "illegal shipments," "duplicated reports," and "discrepancies in testing methods" (U.S. Food and Drug Administration, 2008c).

[17]ERS could only find a Chinese version of this list on the AQSIQ web site.

[18]The blacklist of food product exporters also included listings for many cosmetic products. Only 20 blacklist companies were identified as exporters to Japan, China's largest market for food exports.

Third-Party Certification

China has differing food safety certification systems for domestic and exported food. Food producers serving the domestic market are under

Profile of a Chinese Fish Exporter

Fuzhou Kangdeli Fisheries Co., Ltd., is listed on the AQSIQ web site as an exporter of basa fish. The company lists its main products as roast eel, fish fillets, and octopus. It exports to Japan, the United States, South Korea, Singapore, and Europe. The Fuzhou region is the source of many refused shipments of fish, but we did not find this company's name on FDA import refusal reports. The company's investment is 30 million yuan ($4.4 million), and it is a subsidiary of another company. Photos of the processing plant show clean facilities, modern equipment, and workers with appropriate protective clothing.

The company web site displays copies of several certificates:

- A Hazard Analysis and Critical Control Point (HACCP) certificate was awarded by the provincial CIQ. It specifies that the certificate is for export to the United States (HACCP is required for fish to be sold in the United States) and specifies the product as frozen roasted eel, but basa is specified on the AQSIQ listing.

- A sanitation certificate awarded by the Chinese Government's accreditation agency states: "After audits, your unit complies with requirements for companies exporting food."

- A certificate for ISO-9001:2000 was awarded by CQC (China Quality Center).

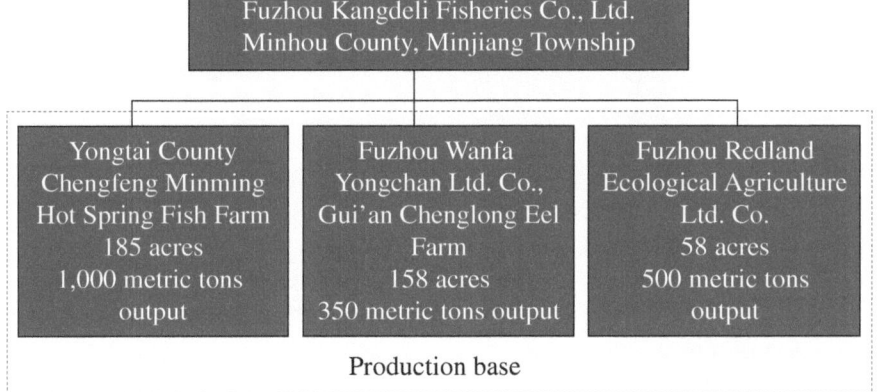

Production base

The "production base" approved to supply Fuzhou Kangdeli listed on the AQSIQ site appears to consist of three separate companies. Some English names had misspellings and questionable translations that could cause confusion. The suppliers are reported to have areas ranging from 58 acres to 185 acres, but it is not clear whether these companies operate their own farms or serve as intermediaries that procure fish from dozens of small farms or fishermen.

The names of the suppliers on the AQSIQ list do not match the suppliers shown on the company web site. One photo on the company site captioned "procuring raw materials" shows a harbor with dozens of small fishing boats. Other photos show a complex of aging concrete aerated ponds, a series of nets for cultivating fish in a natural body of water, and several plastic-covered structures in a valley. (The English- and Japanese-language versions of the web sites do not display all of the photos.)

certification programs developed in China and run by government organizations. A "Pollution-Free" (also known as "no harm" or "safe" food) program was introduced in 2001 by the Ministry of Agriculture as a basic food safety system for agricultural products. The program certifies that a contiguous "production base" of farms meets environmental standards and that products meet domestic standards for chemical residues. A "Green Food" certification was introduced in the 1990s as an early attempt to offer farm products that meet higher overseas standards. Green Food products are exported and sold as premium products in the domestic market. Food processors and manufacturers are required to obtain a "QS" (quality-safety) certification administered by provincial technical supervision bureaus. The QS certification was introduced in 2002 by AQSIQ, which checks the facility's environment, equipment, personnel, plant layout, sources of raw materials, and monitoring capability.

Food exporters—usually processing or manufacturing companies—typically obtain internationally recognized safety certifications like Hazard Analysis and Critical Control Point (HACCP), Good Manufacturing Practices (GMP), and ISO 9001 (in addition to domestic certifications) that are demanded by foreign customers or required by regulations in importing countries (Buzby, 2003). The Chinese Government now requires exporters of meat, poultry, fish, frozen foods, and canned food products to obtain HACCP certification since it is required in many overseas markets. The Organic Food Development Center, affiliated with China's Environmental Protection Agency, is accredited internationally as an organic certifier, and some international organizations also certify organic products in China. China's national accreditation agency has developed standards for Good Agricultural Practices (GAP) in partnership with GLOBALGAP, and Chinese authorities are promoting GAP pilot programs for exporters of medicinal crops, dairy, vegetables, and other produce (Cadilhon and Hoejskov). About 2,800 Chinese food companies have attained HACCP certification and about 300 are certified for GAP. Most of these firms are exporters that typically have modern facilities, equipment, and management practices.[19] Most Chinese food companies—those serving the domestic market—lack the prerequisite facilities, equipment, and well-designed production processes needed to effectively implement HACCP (Zhang and Zhao).

Companies using HACCP or GAP are certified and periodically audited by a third-party organization that sends experienced professionals to assess the company's plans, inspect facilities, make recommendations, and confirm that the management system is properly implemented. Usually companies can choose from a pool of third-party certifiers—companies, governmental body, or nongovernmental organizations—that have gained accreditation from the relevant government or industry body.

In China, certifications and lab tests are performed mainly by government or government-affiliated organizations (Ye). Domestic "pollution-free" and "QS" certifications are performed by organizations affiliated with provincial agricultural or technical supervision bureaus. The sanitation certification for exporters is conducted by a team of provincial CIQ auditors, and products are tested by CIQ. Only a few private-sector certifiers and labs have been accredited to work in China.

[19]Yang noted that some food exporters' operations were disrupted because the companies were not able to integrate multiple management systems, such as HACCP and ISO 9000. Wang et al. describe the experience of a poultry company in implementing HACCP.

HACCP certification for Chinese exporters is performed by provincial quarantine bureaus. CQC, China's largest certification agency, also performs HACCP certifications, as well as organic, GAP, ISO 9000, and other certifications. CQC is nominally an independent entity but was a branch of AQSIQ until 2002. Wang and Ren concluded that water quality testing in China was beset by technical problems, funding and manpower shortages, and selective testing or manipulation of data by officials. Both overseas and domestic consumers might have greater confidence in Chinese food products if a wider range of certifiers and labs were given greater latitude to operate in China. Overseas consumers might have more confidence in government-sponsored tests and certifications if their results could be verified by private-sector third parties.

U.S.-China Consultations

FDA, USDA, and other government agencies have been involved in technical exchanges and training designed to disseminate best practices in food safety to Chinese regulators and producers. Exchanges intensified following the extensive publicity surrounding import safety problems during 2007. In December 2007, U.S. Department of Health and Human Services (which includes FDA) and China's AQSIQ announced an agreement on the safety of food and feed (Becker, 2008a; U.S. Food and Drug Administration, 2008c) and agreed to take the following actions:

- Work to use AQSIQ registration and certification processes on certain high-risk products intended for import to the United States so that FDA can use such registration and certification to inform decisions on the admissibility of products.

- Strengthen AQSIQ's commitment to facilitating timely access for FDA inspectors to Chinese firms, especially during emergency situations.

- Establish joint training programs for food safety inspectors and laboratory technicians.

- Establish a food traceability system in China.

- Require mutual notification by each country of product safety problems, food recalls, and other situations affecting public health.

In implementing the Agreement, FDA and AQSIQ have worked to increase their collaboration in the area of science- and risk-based safety systems, engaged in consultations on standards for lab testing, and begun work under the auspices of working groups on aquatic products and ingredients. In November 2008, FDA opened its China Office, which represented its first-ever overseas office. The China-U.S. agreement may improve the information available to U.S. regulators by establishing systems for China's CIQs to electronically forward company information and test results before shipments arrive at U.S. ports. AQSIQ's information system may eventually develop trace-back capabilities to enable it to better identify sources of food-safety problems.

Conclusions and Discussion

The rapid increase in food imports from China—and their resilience even after widespread negative publicity—reflects the robust demand for these products. It is in the interest of U.S. consumers and Chinese suppliers to find ways to ensure a flow of safe products from China. Regulators and business leaders face stiff challenges in finding creative solutions to facilitate trade between countries with differing agricultural and legal systems.

There are no simple solutions to addressing the safety hazards since they appear to occur in many different types of foods at all links in the supply chain. The difficulty of addressing problems is highlighted by two high-profile food safety incidents—Chinese dumplings adulterated with toxic pesticide in Japan and infant formula adulterated with melamine—that occurred in 2008 after widespread publicity and tightened food safety vigilance in 2007. The incidents occurred in products of companies with well-known brands, HACCP certifications, and official Chinese "inspection-exempt" status.

Safer imported food from China and other overseas sources is likely to entail higher costs. Zhang and Zhao urged Chinese food companies to build in substantial "food safety" costs—investments in sanitary facilities, equipment, water treatment, worker hygiene, changes in production processes, and third-party certifications. A Chinese poultry company studied by Wang et al. (2009) incurred substantial initial investments and higher operating costs to implement a HACCP system. Maintaining laboratories, employing trained technicians, treating water, and complying with environmental regulations raise operating costs. Many exporting firms already have made such investments, but most Chinese firms have little access to capital, operate on thin profit margins, and frequently cut corners to generate profits in China's fiercely competitive food industry. Similarly, some Chinese farms operate according to best practices, but these operations generally require higher investment and operating costs than those of conventional Chinese farms. China's restriction on the potential pool of suppliers by requiring rigorous certification and eliminating contaminated farmland and water from food and fish production reduce the flexibility of companies in choosing suppliers and sourcing raw materials, which also raises costs. As safety-related regulations place constraints on Chinese suppliers, China's cost advantage may be eroded to some degree.

Exported products often bring a higher price than those sold on the domestic Chinese market because of the higher costs of strict safety controls and the large differential between domestic and world prices (Gale and Tuan; Huang and Gale). Because the difference in price is so wide, producers have strong incentives to sell inferior products for export produced at lower cost with fewer safety controls, which creates a challenge in policing supply chains to ensure that unsafe products are excluded.

Private-sector decisionmakers may need to take costly steps that include closer relationships with Chinese suppliers, regular audits, third-party certifications, and independent testing of products. Reportedly, U.S. companies increased their testing of Chinese products (Schwartz) and audits of

Chinese suppliers (Newman) following the adverse publicity regarding food safety in 2007. The difficulty of conducting reliable company audits in China is highlighted by Harney's description of "shadow factories," sophisticated strategies to falsify records, and other means of evading audits by foreign customers.[20]

Consultations and exchanges between U.S. and Chinese officials on food safety are an important step toward a more coordinated safety/quality control system between the two countries (Ellis and Turner). Increased interactions may promote each country's understanding of the counterpart's food safety requirements and differing approaches to food safety control. Food safety has been heavily promoted in China since 2002, but Chinese regulators, farmers, and private decisionmakers are still learning about international safety standards and practices.

Training is helpful in raising awareness of standards and good practices. Lack of experience and training may hamper the effectiveness of personnel who perform laboratory testing, certifications, and audits. Informing industry participants is especially challenging given the high turnover customary among private-sector workers and fluid rates of entry and exit in China's agricultural and food sectors. Training programs in China often reach only technical workers in government organizations; getting information to workers on factory floors and farmers in the field is a challenge. Officials in China have developed web sites, published books, and produced videos on food safety standards and practices for farmers.[21] Government "demonstration projects" post descriptions of safety standards and practices on signboards in fields and greenhouses. Given China's weak agricultural extension service, Chinese officials rely on an "agricultural industrialization" strategy in which agribusiness enterprises transmit technical and market information to farmers, but recent field surveys have found virtually no evidence of farmers receiving technical information from companies (Huang et al., 2008).

Thompson and Hu point out the importance of working with China's provincial officials on food safety oversight issues. Central government officials set general policies, but it is typically up to local officials to carry them out. China has sought to centralize export food safety by putting provincial CIQs directly under the authority of the central AQSIQ (domestic food safety bureaus are under provincial authorities), but local officials still have significant responsibilities and autonomy. For example, the CIQ in Shandong Province (the main source of vegetable exports) implemented a provincial "green card" system to improve vegetable safety following a series of rejections for excessive pesticide residues in Japan. Thompson and Hu emphasize that Hong Kong designed its food import program through consultations with Guangdong Provincial authorities.

Initial U.S.-China consultations have focused on fish and shellfish products, the category that stands out with the most problems. Filth and other common problems, such as dangerous additives and labeling problems, appear to be introduced in the processing of products. Training processors in safe food handling practices and U.S. labeling requirements, clearly specifying allowable additives in contracts, conducting surprise inspections and audits, and requiring third-party certifications may address frequently encountered problems.

[20]Harney discusses audits focused on labor practices, but her discussion applies to food safety audits as well.

[21]It is not clear whether farmers use these materials. Anecdotal and limited survey evidence indicates that farmers in China seldom read newspapers or magazines and few have Internet access; they get most of their information from television.

References

Acheson, David. "Food Safety and Food Imports from China," Testimony to Committee on Appropriations, Subcommittee on Agriculture, Rural Development, Food and Drug Administration, and Related Agencies, U.S. House of Representatives, Tuesday, September 25, 2007, accessed at http://www.dhhs.gov/asl/testify/2007/09/t20070925c.html.

Becker, Geoffrey S. *Food and Agricultural Imports from China*, Congressional Research Service report for Congress, updated January 2, 2008a, accessed at http://www.nationalaglawcenter.org/assets/crs/RL34080.pdf.

Becker, Geoffrey S. *U.S. Food and Agricultural Imports: Safeguards and Selected Issues*, Congressional Research Service Report for Congress, updated April 16, 2008b, accessed at http://opencrs.cdt.org/document/RS22664.

Buzby, Jean C., Laurian J. Unnevehr, and Donna Roberts. *Food Safety and Imported Food: An Analysis Using USFDA Import Refusal Reports*, Economic Information Bulletin No. 39, U.S. Department of Agriculture, Economic Research Service, September 2008.

Buzby, Jean (ed.) *International Trade and Food Safety: Economic Theory and Case Studies*, Agricultural Economic Report No. 828, U.S. Department of Agriculture, Economic Research Service, November 2003, accessed at http://www.ers.usda.gov/publications/aer828/.

Cadilhon, Jean-Joseph, and Peter Sousa Hoejskov. *Quality Standards for Fruits, Vegetables and Pork Meat in China and Hong Kong*, Working document from the Food and Agriculture Organization rapid appraisal mission, Regional Office for Asia and the Pacific, Food and Agriculture Organization of the United Nations, March 2008, accessed October 5, 2008, at ftp://ftp.fao.org/docrep/fao/010/ai416e/ai416e00.pdf.

Calvin, Linda, Fred Gale, Dinghuan Hu, and Bryan Lohmar. "Food Safety Improvements Underway in China," *Amber Waves* 4(5):16-21, U.S. Department of Agriculture, Economic Research Service, November 2006.

China Central Television. "*Bianle Weide Haiwei (Seafood with Altered Taste)*," Weekly Quality Report, November 29, 2004, transcript available at http://news.enorth.com.cn/system/2004/11/29/000913795.shtml, accessed October 5, 2008.

China Food Industry Net. "Aquaculture Product Export Growth Rate Slows in 2007 and Development Faces Challenges," News report, September 3, 2008, accessed at http://agri.gov.cn/fxycpd/xcp/t20080903_1126060.htm.

China Ministry of Foreign Trade and Commerce. *Agricultural Product Export Development Plan for 11th 5-year Plan*, August 2006.

China National Bureau of Statistics. *Rural Statistical Yearbook 2006*, Beijing: China Statistics Press, 2006.

China State Council. *The Quality and Safety of Food in China*, White Paper, August 2007.

Dong, Fengxia, and Helen Jensen. "The Challenge of Conforming to Sanitary and Phytosanitary Measures for China's Agricultural Exports," *Choices* 22(1):19-24, 1st quarter 2007.

Ellis, Linden J., and Jennifer L.Turner. *Sowing the Seeds: Opportunities for U.S.-China Cooperation on Food Safety*, Woodrow Wilson International Center for Scholars China Environment Forum, September 2008.

England, Benjamin L. "Import Operations, Policies, and Procedures," Presentation by the Regulatory Counsel to the Associate Commissioner for Regulatory Affairs, U.S. Food and Drug Administration, October 27, 2000, accessed on March 3, 2008, at www.FDA.gov/oia/embslides/impor-tops/sld001.htm.

Food & Water Watch. *Import Alert: Government Fails Consumers, Falls Short on Seafood Inspections*, Washington, DC, May 2007.

Gale, Fred, Belem Avendaño, and Pierre Merel. *Developing and Improving Techniques and Strategies to Promote Food Safety*, USDA Scientific Exchange Program Trip Report, 2007.

Gale, Fred, and Francis Tuan. *China Currency Appreciation Could Boost U.S. Agricultural Exports*, WRS-0703, U.S. Department of Agriculture, Economic Research Service, August 2007, accessed at http://www.ers.usda.gov/publications/WRS0703/.

Harney, Alexandra. *The China Price: The True Cost of Chinese Competitive Advantage*, New York: Penguin Press, 2008.

Huang, J., Y. Wu, H. Zhi, and S. Rozelle. "Small Holder Incomes, Food Safety and Producing and Marketing China's Fruit," *Review of Agricultural Economics* 30(3):469-79, Fall 2008.

Huang, Sophia, and Fred Gale. *China's Rising Fruit and Vegetable Exports Challenge U.S. Industries*, FTS-32001, U.S. Department of Agriculture, Economic Research Service, February 2006, accessed at http://www.ers.usda.gov/Publications/fts/2006/02feb/fts32001/.

Jerardo, Andy. "What Share of U.S. Consumed Food Is Imported?" *Amber Waves* 6(1):36-37, U.S. Department of Agriculture, Economic Research Service, February 2008.

Kraemer, Don. Testimony before U.S.-China Economic and Security Review Commission Hearing on Chinese Seafood: Safety and Trade Issues, April 25, 2008, accessed at http://www.FDA.gov/ola/2008/seafood042408.html.

Nelson, Stacey, and Suguro Sato. *Update on MRL Violations in Japan 2007*, GAIN Report No. JA7009, U.S. Department of Agriculture, Foreign Agricultural Service, March 2007, accessed at http://www.fas.usda.gov/gainfiles/200703/146280598.pdf.

Newman, Douglas. "Canned Fruit: China Field Notes," Unpublished trip report, U.S. International Trade Commission, September 2007.

Sanchez, Jorge, Tanya C. Franke, and Amy Zecha. *U.S. Seafood Exports to China are Re-Exported to Third Countries*, GAIN Report No. CH8005, U.S. Department of Agriculture, Foreign Agricultural Service, January 2008, accessed at http://www.fas.usda.gov/gainfiles/200808/146295431.pdf.

Schmit, Julie. "U.S. Food Imports Outrun USFDA Resources," *USA Today*, March 18, 2007.

Schwartz, Nelson. "Companies in U.S. Increase Testing of Chinese Goods," *New York Times*, July 1, 2007.

Schönmann, Jochen. "China Being Poisoned by its Food Industry, Says Author," *Der Spiegel,* December 18, 2007, accessed at http://www.spiegel.de/international/world/0,1518,523988,00.html.

Sun, Xiaohua. "SEPA Sets Sights on Polluted Soil," *China Daily,* January 9, 2008.

Thompson, Drew, and Hu Ying. "Food Safety in China: New Strategies," *Global Health Governance* 1(2):1-9, December 2007.

Ting, Cheng. "Thailand Finds Carcinogens in Imported Chinese Produce," Radio Free Asia, August 23, 2007.

Unnevehr, L.J. "Food Safety Issues and Fresh Food Product Exports from LDCs, *Agricultural Economics* 23(3):231-40, September 2000.

U.S. Congress. *Food from China: Can We Import Safely?* Subcommittee on Oversight and Investigations, staff trip report, September 2007.

U.S. Food and Drug Administration. Data on the numerous individual import alerts can be obtained from the FDA Import Alert Retrieval System (FIARS), accessed January 2008a at http:// www.FDA.gov/ora/fiars/ora_import_alerts.html.

U.S. Food and Drug Administration. "Detention Without Physical Examination of Aquacultured Catfish, Basa, Shrimp, Dace, and Eel Products from the People's Republic of China Due to the Presence of New Drugs and/or Unsafe Food Additives," Import Alert 16-131, August 8, 2007a, accessed at http://www.FDA.gov/ora/fiars/ora_import_ia16131.html.

U.S. Food and Drug Administration. "Detention Without Physical Examination of all Vegetable Protein Products From China for Animal or Human Food Use Due to the Presence of Melamine and/or Melamine Analogs," Import Alert 99-29, July 31, 2007b, accessed at http://www.FDA.gov/ora/fiars/ora_import_ia9929.html.

U.S. Food and Drug Administration. *Food Protection Plan: An Integrated Strategy for Protecting the Nation's Food Supply*, November 2007c, accessed on February 28, 2008, at http://www.FDA.gov/oc/initiatives/advance/food/plan.html.

U.S. Food and Drug Administration. Home page for "Operational and Administrative System for Import Support (OASIS)," October 28, 2004, accessed January 2008b at http://www.FDA.gov/ora/import/oasis/home_page.html.

U.S. Food and Drug Administration. "Joint Progress Statement Regarding the Five-Year Work Plan Under the Agreement on the Safety of Food and Feed," June 2008c, accessed at http://www.FDA.gov/bbs/topics/news/international/progress_HHS_China.pdf.

U.S. Food and Drug Administration. "Questions and Answers on FDA's Import Alert on Farm-Raised Seafood From China," June 28, 2007d, accessed at http://www.cfsan.FDA.gov/~frf/seadwpe.html.

Wang, Shijie, Huili Duan, Wei Zhang, and Jun-Wen Li. "Analysis of Bacterial Foodborne Disease Outbreaks in China Between 1994 and 2005," *FEMS Immunology and Medical Microbiology* 51(1):8-13, October 2007.

Wang, Yichao, and Bo Ren. "Waking Up to China's Water Crisis," *Caijing*, web edition, September 12, 2007.

Wang, Zhigang, Huina Yuan, and Fred Gale. "Costs of Adopting HACCP: Case Study of a Chinese Poultry Processing Firm." *Review of Agricultural Economics*, forthcoming 2009.

Weise, Elizabeth. "China's Budding Food Industry Faces Scrutiny," *USAToday*, May 22, 2007.

Wong, S.C., X.D. Li, G. Zhang, S.H. Qi, and Y.S. Min. "Heavy Metals in Agricultural Soils of the Pearl River Delta, South China," *Environmental Pollution* 119:33-44, 2002.

Wu, Yongning. "Food Safety in China: Where Do We Stand?" Presentation at Woodrow Wilson Center China Environmental Forum, Washington DC, December 2007.

Yang, Chengsuo. "Strengthen Sanitation Supervision for Food Export Enterprises." (in Chinese) *China Inspection and Quarantine Times*, 02 December 2008, p. 4. accessed April 2, 2009 at http://cngm.cqn.com.cn.

Ye, Zhihua. "Investigation on Third Party Certification for Food Safety in China," Presentation at International Symposium on Food Traceability, Beijing, October 2007.

Zhang, Dingdong, and Guilin Zhao. "Chukou Shipin Qiye HACCP Tixi Yingyongde Cunzai Wenti he Duice (Problems and Measures for Food-exporting Enterprises That Must Use the HACCP System)," (in Chinese) Presentation, October 11, 2006, accessed June 4, 2008 at http://www.cnca.gov.cn/rjwzcjgb/haccp/yt/images/20061011/338.ppt.